Brooks Field
Autzen Stadium

LEGEND
- Donor Reserved Parking
- Donor RV Parking
- Accessible Parking

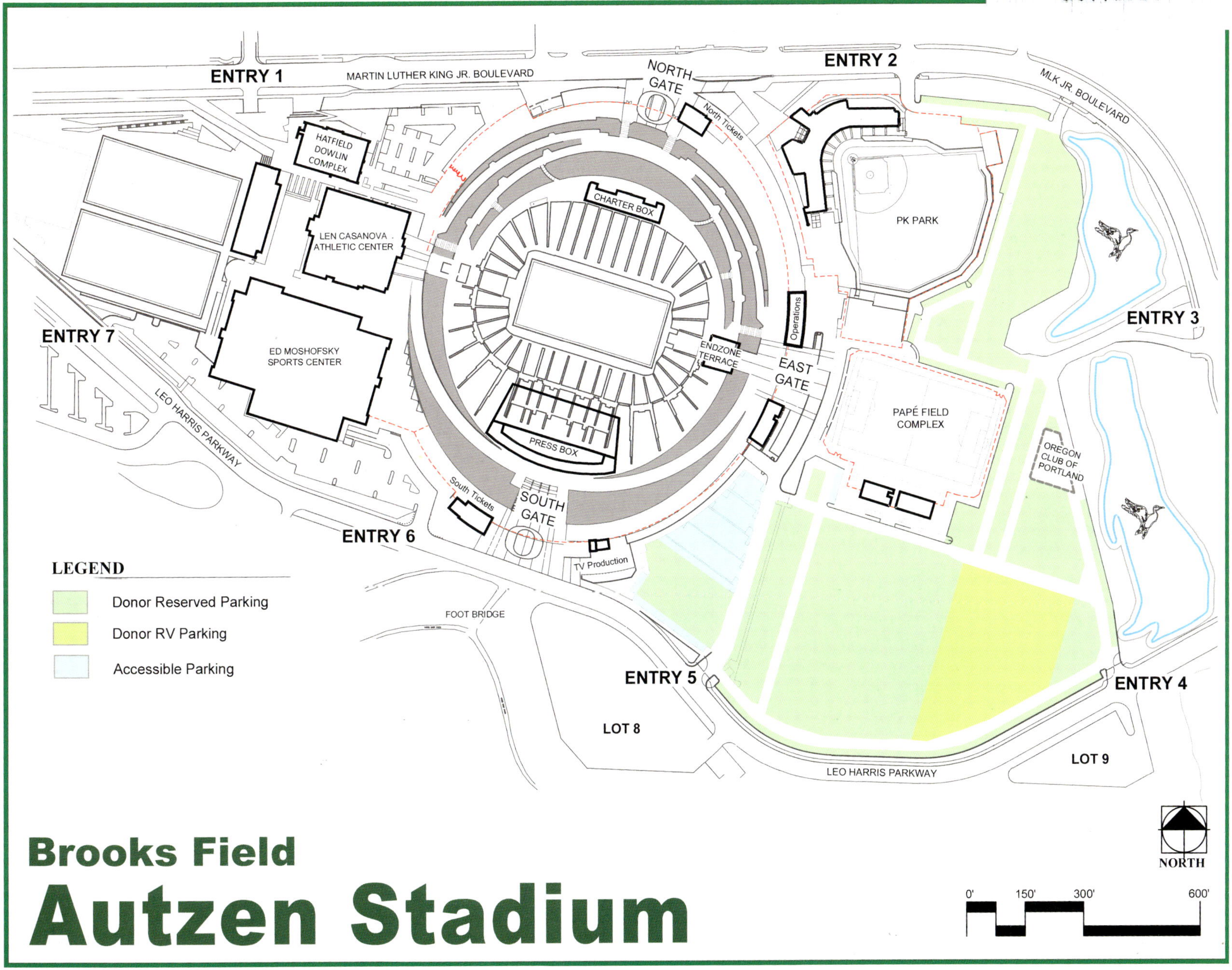

Courtesy of the Oregon athletic department

GAME DAY
with the
OREGON DUCKS

An Insider's Look at a UO Football Game

Written by Robert Young   Photographs by Jack Liu

For curious Duck fans everywhere

Text Copyright © 2016 by Robert Young
Photographs Copyright © 2016
by QSL Print Communications

All rights reserved. No part of this book may be reproduced, stored in a retrieval system, or transmitted in any form or by any means whatsoever without the prior written permission of QSL Print Communications, except for the inclusion of brief quotations in an acknowledged review.

Published by Koke Next Generation, Inc.
Springfield, Oregon

Library of Congress Control Number:
2016946726
ISBN: 978-0-692-73748-4

Printed in the United States of America
QSL Print Communications
3000 Pierce Parkway
Springfield, Oregon 97477

ACKNOWLEDGMENTS

Like a successful football program, a successful book takes support and teamwork. The author would like to thank the following people for helping in the creation of this book:

Jerry Allen, Vicky Allard, Logan Anderson, Jeff Baden, Jerry Bishop, Chris Bjork, Blaire Buckley, Ben Camel, Lisa Cannell, Daniel Cook, Derrick Cook, Ben Creighton, Brian Davies, Chris Davis, Marcus Davis, Timm Dotson, Dennis Eastburn, Greg Erickson and his sixth grade class, Osbaldo Escatel, Taryn Fahoury, Kenny Farr, Hugh Fullagar, Stephanie Fuller, Gemineye, Steve Greatwood, Rodney Hardrick, Jason Harris, Joe Hass, Britnie Jones, Sam Kamkar, Scott LaBounty, Marcus Lee, Malik Lovette, John Lundquist, Chris Malme, Scott Martin, Johnie Mathews and his sixth grade class, Mike Maulding, Terry McCabe, Andy McNamara, Austin Meek, Kwame Mitchell, Ethan Mohr, Joe Motta, Phil Neri, Khalil Oliver, Pratik Patel, Curt Parks, Alicia Perkins, Jake Pisarcik, Jim Radcliffe, Micha Ray, Kevin Rice, Megan Robertson, Tony Rodriguez, Johnny Rogers, John Sargeant, Jay Shadwick, Devon Shea, Dwayne Stanford, Kevin Steil, Vicki Strand, Teresa Sutten, Jody Sykes, Steve Tannen, Kim Terrell, Roger Toy, Will Turner and Cheeto, Anna Waite, Aaron Wasson, Austin Werking, Mitch Wofford, and Neil Zoumboukos.

The professionals at QSL have done an outstanding job creating a book out of words and photographs. Thanks to Jennifer Fairbanks, Sandy Toney, Karen McClinton, Jen Spires, and the entire production team.

Special thanks to Tyler Young, Jerry Thompson and Tom Reichert for helping launch this project, to Doug and Melissa Koke for believing in an idea, to Dave Williford for providing key contacts, to Craig Pintens for reviewing the manuscript, to Jack Liu for his cooperation as well as outstanding photographs, and to Ava Litton for her love, support, and assistance every step of the way.

Game Day with the Oregon Ducks

Before

Morning fog silently sits in Autzen Stadium.

Later today, nearly 60,000 people will pack the seats and fill the air with shouts and cheers as they watch the Oregon Ducks play. Fans in the stands won't be the only ones to experience the game. A million and a half people will watch the game on their TVs or computer screens. Several million more will listen on their radios.

The University of Oregon sports complex looks empty, but it is not. Some of the two thousand people who will work at the game today have already arrived. The events director has checked in with overnight security guards, unlocked doors, and inspected the area. Food service managers have met to do their final planning. The equipment administrator has assembled his staff and assigned duties.

Autzen Stadium was named after Thomas J. Autzen (1888-1958), an Oregon State graduate and plywood manufacturer from Portland. Autzen's foundation, under the direction of his son, donated $250,000—the largest single donation—to help build the stadium in 1966. The stadium opened on September 23, 1967.

The playing field—Brooks Field—was named after Rich Brooks, who coached the team from 1977 to 1994.

One duty of the equipment staff is to post the warm-up schedule for the team. Duck players will enter the field by position groups. Each group, led by a coach, follows a schedule, timed to the minute.

A mile-and-a-half away in the kitchen at Matthew Knight arena, the smell of turkey drifts through the air. Here, food staff roasts meat, mixes barbecue sauces, and makes macaroni and cheese to sell at the game. Trucks with "hot boxes," insulated containers, will deliver the food to the stadium. Across town, a private catering company prepares food for the suites that line the stadium high above the field.

There are 40 sky suites at Autzen Stadium. Each has a kitchen, bathroom, TVs, and windows that open. These suites hold between 21 and 44 people, and are leased for three to seven years. The cost: $40,000 to $90,000 a year.

The equipment staff is responsible for the footballs the Ducks use on game day. Ten to twelve balls will be available during the game.

Back at Autzen, Duck Store workers roll out racks of clothing and bins of hats, blankets, gloves and other merchandise from a storage pod. They will stock the shelves of their booth outside the stadium and be ready when the parking lots open.

Nearby, a TV crew unloads trailers that carry their equipment. They haul the equipment inside the stadium.

Preparing cables for TV cameras

Skycam is a camera that "flies" over the field giving unique views of the game. The 50-pound camera hangs from four, 1,400-foot long metal cables attached to towers at the corners of the stadium.

An engineer strides to the middle of the field and tests Skycam, which has taken several days to install at the stadium. The Skycam will be one of nine cameras the television crew will use. The crew assembles cameras and microphones then connects them to cables that run to a large trailer that sits outside the stadium. From inside this trailer, the TV crew will produce the national broadcast for viewers.

More cameras will be used during the game: four for DuckVision, the video shown on the stadium scoreboard, and three more to record the action for the coaching staff to review and evaluate the game. Local news sportscasters will carry cameras to film highlights for their news programs.

A small group of staff and players select the uniforms months before the football season begins. Designers from Nike present options to the group, which then makes its choices. The head coach has the final approval. Many different "looks" are possible because the Ducks have many parts to choose from: five different helmets (with a variety of decals), seven jerseys, six pants, five cleats, eight socks, and five gloves. That's at least 42,000 different uniform possibilities!

Phil Knight, co-founder of Nike, is a UO graduate and former student-athlete. Over the years, he and his wife, Penny, have donated more than $300 million to the university and athletic department. Knight has been honored with his own locker in the Ducks' locker room. The front of the locker reads: Uncle Phil.

While the Duck players still sleep at a local hotel, the equipment staff prepares the locker room. Getting uniforms ready for 105 players on game day is a weekly challenge. Luckily, a lot of the work was already done.

During the week leading up to the game, the 12 equipment workers placed the smaller parts of the uniforms—socks, tights, gloves, t-shirts—into laundry loops, mesh pouches with zippers. They placed those loops in players' lockers. On game day, the workers remove shoulder pads from the lockers and put them inside of the uniform tops. The sports scientist has already taped Global Positioning System (GPS) units onto the shoulder pads. The units, which use satellite technology, will collect important information about the players during the game.

Equipment staff prepares the locker room for the players. The helmets will be placed along the bench, and all will face the playing field.

GPS unit being taped onto shoulder pads

Headsets await the Duck coaches.

Music fills the air inside the stadium as the Oregon Marching Band prepares for today's game. Under the watchful eye of the director, the 235 band members rehearse for their halftime show. They have already practiced nearly eight hours this week and will add two more hours this morning. The halftime show will last only six to eight minutes!

While the band plays on, workers set up communication systems around the field. Near the east end zone, a man prepares the wireless microphone the referee wears to communicate with viewers and listeners. On the Ducks' sideline, two men prepare the coaches headsets they will wear to speak with each other during the game.

The equipment and athletic training staffs wheel carts and benches onto the sideline. Some of the carts hold extra equipment—helmet parts, tools, and extra pads—the staff might need during the game. Other carts hold large containers of fluids—water and sports drinks—for the team. Players sit on the benches, heated by propane, to stay warm during cold weather. The benches can dry their helmets and warm their feet, too.

Workers also set out the special teams' mat as well as a portable bathroom. Coaches use the mat to organize their special teams—punting, kickoff, field goal—during the game. Players stand on the mat by position when the coach calls for the team.

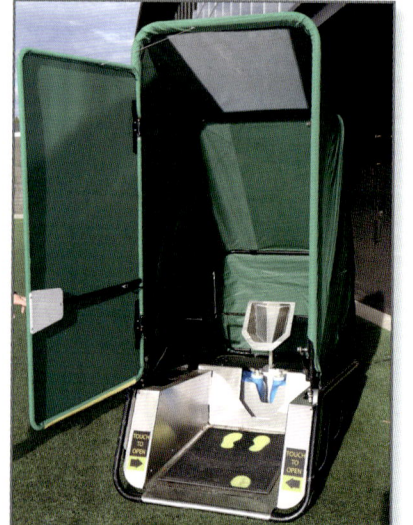

This special bathroom automatically sets up when a player steps on the floor and collapses after a specified time.

Wearing blue jackets, the 540 members of the event staff arrive at the stadium in waves. First come the men and women who help with parking in the lots around the stadium. Next come the ticket workers. The people who serve as ushers and security guards inside the stadium arrive closer to game time.

A supervisor meets with each group and goes over details the workers need to know.

By now, the Duck coaches have awakened the players. They dress then board a bus that police escort to the Hatfield-Dowlin Complex. In the cafeteria, the players, coaches, and staff eat their pre-game meals. The nutritionist has carefully selected the meal. It includes chicken, steak, pasta, rice, green vegetables, salad, and lots of fresh fruit. While the players eat, the nutrition staff walks around and helps players make good food choices.

Eating the right foods is important for the Ducks to play their best. The nutritionist assesses the food needs of every player at the beginning of the season. He creates an eating plan for each one and monitors it all season long.

While the players eat, activity around the stadium picks up. Vehicles begin streaming into the parking areas. In the Moshofsky (Mo) Center, concession workers prepare their sales areas while the marketing staff pumps up the giant inflatables. In an office near the Mo Center, ticket staff collects the 100 machines they will use to scan tickets. Event staff drive out trams that will shuttle people around the stadium.

Cheerleaders warm-up and rehearse their routines in the Mo Center.

The Moshofsky Center, completed in 1998, was the first indoor practice facility on the West Coast. The Ducks use the 117,000 square foot space to improve their skills on its artificial turf. For game days, a crew of fourteen lays down a portable floor. The floor takes five-and-a-half hours to install.

High above the field in the press box, the football communications director has posted the seating order for the people who will be watching the game from the open seating area. Most will be reporters and writers. Some will be scouts from professional teams. In a room nearby, a facilities technician uses three different passwords to log onto his computer. He checks the program that automatically controls most of the areas that heat and light the stadium. He'll monitor these throughout the day.

By now, the fog has lifted from the stadium and the team has moved to meeting rooms for their "clap sessions." With the players seated in different formations, a coach calls out a play, everyone claps their hands in rhythm, then the players point to the person or area they are responsible for.

Inside the stadium, workers prepare the special seating areas—sky suites, club level, Charter Box, and Endzone Terrace—for the game. Some of the 1,200 volunteers who will run the food booths report and begin counting their inventory.

In a small room below the Charter Box, a young man operates a popcorn machine. As the machine fills with popcorn, he empties it into large bags. He'll finish filling 120 bags for the game today, and workers will deliver the bags to sales areas around the stadium.

The Ducks have 75-80 plays in their plan for each game.

Ticket staff opens their offices on the north and south ends of the stadium. People can buy tickets to the game, or pick up tickets they have already purchased. If they've lost their tickets, new ones can be printed.

When security guards open the gates, Duck fans flock into the Mo Center. Soon, the band begins playing the Oregon Fight Song, and the mascot leads coaches, players, and football staff on their March to Victory. With smiles, waves, and high-fives, the team greets enthusiastic fans before heading to their locker room in the Hatfield-Dowlin Complex.

The original mascot was a real-life duck named "Puddles." The university used "Puddles" and other live ducks until the 1940s, when the Humane Society complained about the way the ducks were treated. In 1947, the athletic director got permission from Walt Disney to use the likeness of Donald Duck as the mascot. It's been used ever since, and is named The Duck.

From there, the players walk down a flight of stairs to the training area. Here, they will get their bodies ready for the game. Athletic trainers assist by taping players, providing medical treatment, and directing them to facilities and equipment. Some players prepare by sitting or exercising in a warm pool of water. Others use bands or rollers.

When players are done in the training area, they return to the locker room. They are eager to start the game, but there are still a few hours before kickoff. Players fill this time talking, listening to music, or watching TV. Some go out on the field to exercise or play catch. Back in the locker room, the Ducks put on their uniforms. Some apply eye-black or stickers to their faces. All have their helmets checked to make sure they fit properly.

Taping helps provide support as well as prevent injuries.

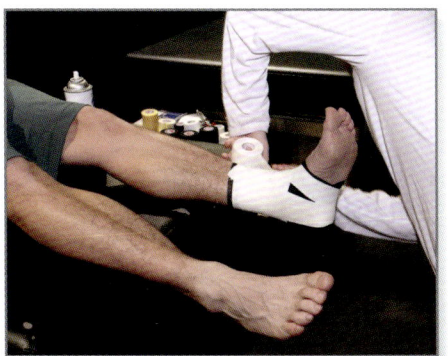

Athletic trainers use about 1,500 yards of athletic tape for each game. That's nearly a mile of tape!

Eye black is a type of grease. Some players use it to reduce glare. Others just like the way it looks. Early eye black was made from burned cork. It was first used in a football game in 1942 by Washington Redskins' fullback Andy Farkas.

The eight officials for the game have arrived and dressed in their locker room inside the stadium. The head official, the referee, will meet with coaches from both teams before the game begins. He wants to know of any special plays or formations the teams might use so that his crew will be in the right positions to do their jobs.

At the opposite end of the stadium, near the east end zone, photographers set up their computers in a long, narrow room. The room is known as "the cave." The photographers will upload the pictures they take onto these computers. After setting up, the photographers make their way up to the press box.

As game time approaches, the media and other workers enjoy a delicious buffet-style meal in the press box. Outside, excited fans have their tickets scanned and move to their seats. Event workers help those who need assistance.

Answer: The one on the right.

Scanning tickets is quick, and it protects against counterfeit tickets, which are difficult to detect by looking at them. Which of these tickets is fake?

In the 2002 game against Mississippi State, the motorcycle rider drove too close to an official, who threw his flag. The Ducks had a penalty before the game even started!

Waiting for the cue from the producer

The Ducks return to their locker room, where the head coach talks to motivate the players to do their best. The team is ready now and walks to the tunnel that leads to the field. In the stadium, music thunders and the crowd cheers as it watches highlights from past games on the scoreboard.

Fog has returned to Autzen, this time made by a machine. Outside the tunnel, The Duck and a driver wait on a motorcycle. When the cue is given, the motorcycle roars to life and leads the team onto the field.

It's game time!

Game Day with the Oregon Ducks

The crowd roars as the Ducks' high-speed offense runs and passes the ball up the field. Eight officials watch closely to make sure the players and coaches follow the rules. When a penalty is called, the referee uses his wireless microphone to announce it.

During

While the main action is on the field, there is plenty going on along the sidelines. Photographers line the field, taking pictures and recording the action. The ball boys race up and down the sidelines, making sure the officials have a football ready for every play. Security workers and police look into the stands, keeping a careful watch on the crowd. The sideline crew, called the "chain gang" helps the officials manage the game.

Overhead, the Skycam zips along its cables at up to twenty miles an hour. Two men use computers to control the camera from a booth in the press box. One man, the pilot, moves the camera along the cables. The operator aims the camera.

The ball boy keeps extra footballs in a bag. When the weather is cold, he places a warmer in the bag. When it rains, he uses a towel to dry the footballs.

Nine people make up the "chain gang." They keep track of what down it is, where the officials should place the ball to start each play, and where the teams need to get for a first down. They take notes on every play, and they place markers along the sidelines to make it easier for the TV workers to place the colored lines they use to show viewers first down yardage.

The two people holding the first down poles are called "stick men." The person holding the down marker pole is called the "box man." The term came from the cube that once sat on top of the marker pole and was rotated to display the down.

Athletic training staff carry packs with medical supplies.

A variety of people join players and coaches gathered on the sidelines. The strength and conditioning staff watch for injuries and help keep the players organized. Athletic trainers and doctors stand ready to assist with injuries. If a player is hurt, the referee stops the game and trainers rush onto the field to assess the player. If the trainers need help, they point to their heads, the signal that means a doctor is needed. Equipment staff replaces bent facemasks, ripped jerseys, or problem shoes. Everyone who can—including the nutrition staff and the sports scientist—offers fluids to the players.

Oregon players sweat out three to ten pounds during a game. Losing more than 2% of body weight in sweat can affect the speed and power of a player. That's four pounds for a 200 pound player. Replacing lost fluids is essential to helping players perform their best. The team drinks up to 100 gallons of fluids on game day.

In the stands, marketing interns find people showing their Duck spirit. The interns radio the "spirit cam" operator to their location, and he shoots live video that gets relayed to the director.

Out on the field, the Ducks' quarterback scrambles away from defenders and looks downfield. A receiver has gotten behind his defender and is wide open! The quarterback lofts the pass into the air, the receiver gathers it in, and races to the end zone.

Touchdown Ducks!

In the announcer's booth, an audio worker pushes a button that plays a recording of a fog horn that is amplified through the twenty-three powerful speakers that line the roof of the Endzone Terrace. Woooooooooooo! The crowd goes wild and the band plays. After the extra point, The Duck drops and begins his push-ups.

"Twenty yards on the carry," booms a voice throughout the stadium. "First down, Ducks!" The voice comes from the announcer sitting in a press box booth. Two assistants help him identify players involved in each play and the yardage gained or lost. Joining them in this busy booth are the scoreboard operators, some of the audio team, and the producer. Through her headset, the producer speaks with the announcer, audio crew, the DJ working in the next booth, the DuckVision director at Matthew Knight arena, and other staff around the stadium. She uses a 40-page script developed during the week to guide the staff through presentations, promotions, and general information.

Other booths in the press box are busy, too. In one booth, an athletic trainer works as a medical spotter. She watches for helmet-to-helmet contact between players, which can cause concussions. She looks for other injuries, too, and uses TV replay to see how the injury happened. Then she relays the information to the head athletic trainer on the sideline so the players can get hands-on help.

The DuckVision director and his crew work in a control room at Matthew Knight arena. He chooses videos, visuals, replays, or live shots to show on the stadium scoreboard. The information is carried along fiber-optic cable that runs from the arena to the stadium.

After each score, The Duck does push-ups to equal the total number of points the team has. In 2010, when Oregon beat New Mexico 72-0, The Duck did 506 push-ups!

Some Oregon coaches work from a press box booth (center). The producer sits in the next booth (left). TV broadcasters work in another booth (right).

Several Oregon coaches sit in another booth. Watching from high above the field, the coaches get a great perspective. They can see what is working well and what is not, and they can share that information with the other coaches. The offensive coach calls plays from here. He communicates the plays to a few players on the sideline wearing headsets. They then pass the plays on to the team by using signs and signals.

In the front row of one of the radio booths, two men—a play-by-play announcer and a color commentator—describe the game to listeners. The announcer talks about what happens on each play. The commentator adds his insights. Between them sits an assistant, and behind them a producer monitors the broadcast.

The assistant keeps careful notes of every play and uses cards to display interesting information for the announcer to share with listeners.

Another booth serves as the instant replay booth, where game officials take a closer look at plays to see if the calls on the field were correct. Workers track game statistics in yet another booth. They enter information about each play into a computer. After every quarter, the information is totaled, printed out, and distributed throughout the press box. Writers and broadcasters share the information with their readers, listeners, and viewers.

Halftime is a great time to discover interesting features of Autzen. Inside the south entrance is art made from the tops of trophies.

At halftime, the Ducks gather in a locker room beneath the stands. While the coaches meet to discuss the game, the players rest, eat energy snacks, and drink fluids. Athletic training staff evaluates injuries and reports them to the coaches. Before halftime ends, the coaches will meet with the players and prepare them for the second half.

While the team rests and prepares, the band performs on the field, photographers upload pictures in "the cave," and fans buy food and drinks around the stadium and at the Mo Center. As the twenty-minute halftime comes to an end, fans hurry back to their seats to wait for the third quarter to begin.

Events director viewing security camera monitors in S.O.S. booth

Game day security is very important. Along with the security staff and local police, a bomb-sniffing dog works to keep everyone safe.

Each game, security and police eject 30 to 100 people from the stadium for breaking rules or laws.

The events director stands in the Stadium Operations Security (S.O.S.) booth of the press box. Around her are a team of men and women who help make game day safe and manageable for all. If there is a problem in or around the stadium, this team will soon know. Then, they will respond to it. This is the command center.

Complaints get reported here, and the team views monitors at the back of the booth to see what the 19 security cameras placed around the stadium are recording. If a person is breaking a rule or law, the police commander uses a radio to dispatch some of the 70 police officers to the scene. If someone is having a health issue, the medical leader radios an American Red Cross First Aid Station Team (FAST). The team assesses the problem and takes care of it if they can. If not, they contact one of the eight teams of paramedics that are nearby to assist. Four ambulances sit outside the stadium for emergencies.

Each FAST is made up of volunteers: high school and college students as well as adults. The American Red Cross provides training to the 80 people in the program. About 25 FAST members attend every home game and are organized into seven teams throughout the stadium.

The sixty food areas have done great business today. They've sold a lot of bottled water, large sodas, popcorn, pretzels, and, of course, hot dogs. By the end of the day, people will buy more than 6,000 bottles of water and nearly 4,500 hot dogs!

A worker wheels more hot dog buns to a food area.

Why is the attendance usually larger than the number of seats in the stadium? It's because the people who bought standing room only tickets are included in the total. So are the people who work at the stadium.

Sales have been good at the seven Duck Stores today. Because of the cold weather, blankets and gloves have been the best sellers. Staff carries more products from storage areas to restock shelves.

By now, most of the ticket staff has finished for the day. A few workers remain in the south gate ticket office and total the attendance for the game. When they are done, they text the number to media in the press box so that it can be recorded and announced. Then, they find a place to watch the rest of the game.

Bottled water was a big hit on September 6, 2014 when the Ducks played Michigan State. On that day, fans bought 22,000 bottles, the most ever at Autzen. What do you think the weather was like?

On the field, the Ducks make another defensive stand. The scoreboard reads:

"MAKE SOME NOISE"

and the crowd responds. The stadium gets louder and louder and louder. The deafening noise keeps the other team from hearing their quarterback call signals. An offensive lineman jumps offsides and the officials call a penalty. On the next play, the Ducks stop the runner short of a first down. The defense has held once more.

Enthusiastic Duck fans make Autzen one of the loudest stadiums in the nation. During the Ducks' win over Michigan in 2007, the noise level was measured at 127.2 decibels. That's louder than a jackhammer or a rock concert!

During the fourth quarter, preparations begin for the end of the game. Police officers move to the streets around the stadium to direct the thousands of vehicles that will soon take to the road. Inside the Mo Center, the marketing staff takes down the inflatables. In the press box, sportswriters begin to write their stories. On the field, photographers try to get their last best shots.

When the scoreboard clock clicks down to zero, the mighty Ducks have won another game!

Oregon is one of the few college teams that allow fans on the field after the game.

Game Day with the Oregon Ducks

After

The game is over, but game day is far from finished.

Players and coaches from both teams fill the field, greeting and congratulating each other. Some form a circle near the 50-yard line to say a prayer. Members of the media ask players questions about the game. As the athletic staff begins to clear the sidelines of supplies and equipment, the Ducks make their way to the locker room, where they hear from the coaches, and sing "Mighty Oregon."

Albert Perfect, the UO band director in 1915, and Dewitt Gilbert, a journalism student, wrote "Mighty Oregon," the school's fight song. The song was first performed on March 4, 1916.

After the players take off their pads, the strength and conditioning coach leads them to the recovery pools, where they walk through the chest-deep water. The first pool is 63 degrees. The water is colder—55 degrees—in the second pool. Brrrrrr! That's almost as cold as the ocean water at the Oregon coast. The cold water helps muscles recover from the game.

In the interview area near the locker room, men and women from the media ask the head coach questions about the game. Soon, some of the Duck players take turns sitting at the front of the room and answering questions. After all the questions have been asked and answered, the players return to their locker room. Some shower and dress. Others visit the training room to get medical help before they shower and dress. Then, the players join their family and friends waiting for them. Coaches meet with recruits and their families.

Families, friends, and fans wait for players outside the Hatfield-Dowlin Complex lobby.

After the interviews, the media return to the stadium and up to the press box. There they will use information from the interviews as well as game statistics to write their stories. TV sportscasters transmit the video they recorded to their news stations. Down in "the cave," photographers upload and sort their pictures as the security staff slowly clears the field of people. As visitors leave the stadium, many stop by one of the Duck Stores. It's their last chance on game day to buy Duck gear.

For local news, sportscasters record 2.5 to 3 hours of video during a game. They will use 90 seconds for their reports and another 40 to 60 seconds for highlights. Two photographers from the local newspaper combine to take 3,000 to 4,000 pictures during the game. Of those, 20 to 30 will be posted online and 8 to 10 will be printed in the newspaper.

In the locker room, the sports scientist removes the GPS units from players' shoulder pads. He takes the units to his office, uploads the information from them onto his computer, and then prints out a report for the coaches. The coaches can use the information to make decisions about training and playing time.

Do you like doing wash? Trying doing it for 120 people! The equipment staff gathers up the uniforms from the players as well as the coaches and puts the clothing into washing machines. It will take hours to wash and dry the 500 pounds of clothes. Then the staff has to sort it all and put it away.

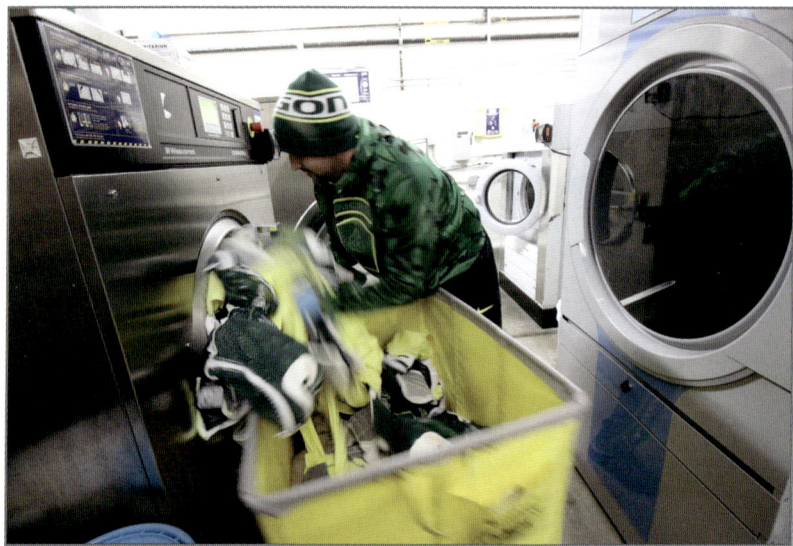

Equipment staff uses five washing machines to clean players' and coaches' clothing.

The GPS units measure the impacts players take during the game as well as the distance they run and their speed. The fastest Duck players run 22-24 miles an hour. The fastest human, Usain Bolt, has run 27.8 miles an hour.

The men and women who set up the sidelines now work to put everything away: TV cameras, cables, microphones, and headsets. The equipment and athletic training staffs roll their carts off to unload and store. The special teams' mat is put away and the portable bathroom is emptied, cleaned, and stored.

In the SOS booth, the events manager meets with her senior staff. What incidents took place during game day? What plans do they need to make for the next game? Other event staff members are working in and around the stadium to help visitors as they leave. Some drive trams or golf carts to help people get to their cars or bus-loading areas. Others help guests retrieve items they've lost during game day.

There is a lot of work to do in the food areas. Some of the volunteers clean and prepare them for the next game. Others count the inventory, total the money collected, and take it to an office in the athletic complex. There, protected by armed guards, food staff and volunteers count the money together. Then, the money is loaded into an armored car, which will take it to be safely deposited.

Volunteers selling food at Duck games represent an organization, like a church or school. The organization receives 8–15% of all sales the volunteers make.

Cleaning up a food booth

Food volunteers gather leftover food, which the UO donates to a local charity.

If the athletic complex were a city on game day, it would be the ninth most populated city in Oregon. What do you get when you put that many people together in a small area during the course of a day? You get garbage, and lots of it!

That makes cleaning up the stadium after a game a massive undertaking. It takes time and a lot of work by many people. Most of the work won't be done on game day. It will begin early tomorrow morning, when the first of up to 500 volunteers and other workers arrive to do the job.

Ten people from the facilities staff will direct the workers as they clean the special seating areas, the bathrooms, and the press box. Inside the stadium, the workers will pick up much of the trash by hand and use blowers along with large vacuums to get the rest. They will dump all the garbage and recycling collected into large containers that will be emptied into garbage trucks and hauled away. After eight hours, Autzen Stadium will be ready for the next game.

Visitors and workers at Autzen Stadium on game day leave behind 52,800 pounds of garbage. That's 26.4 tons! Luckily, not all of that garbage will end up in landfills. Nearly half of it will be recycled.

Near the press box, a facilities technician checks the computer program that controls the heat and lights. The program is still working well, adjusting heat and turning off lights. Facility technicians will shut off most of the other lights, including the field lights when the stadium is empty.

Darkness has dropped into Autzen Stadium.

It will silently sit until the light of morning, when work begins again. Next weekend nearly 60,000 people will pack the stands and fill the air with shouts and cheers as they watch the Oregon Ducks play.

About the Author & Photographer

Robert Young (www.realwriting.us) is a teacher, writing consultant, and the author of twenty-seven books for children. Topics for his books reflect his many interests and curiosities, including history, sports, animals, and people.

When not writing, he enjoys kayaking, hiking, and making author visits to schools as near as Eugene and as far as Buenos Aires.

Originally from the east coast, Robert earned a degree from the University of Oregon and makes his home in the Willamette Valley, near the hawks, trails, and water he loves.

Jack Liu (jackliuphotographer.com) has been taking pictures for the University of Oregon for over 25 years. He was born in Tokyo, Japan and grew up both there and in New York City. He came to Eugene to go to college and received a Bachelors and Master of Fine Arts degree from the University of Oregon.

Jack is a lifelong Duck fan and taking photos of Duck football is a dream come true. In his spare time Jack loves to play his guitar, listen to music, and have fun with his family.